figure 7

figure 8

crimping

To crimp with chainnose pliers, simply mash the crimp as flat as possible, making sure the wires aren't crossed inside the crimp.

Crimping with crimping pliers has two steps. It's also a good idea to place a bead between the crimp and the clasp to ease strain on the wire at the crimp. Make sure you can thread the wire through this bead twice.

Figure 7: On one end of a length of flexible beading wire thread a crimp bead, then a large-hole bead. Go through one end of the clasp. Bring the wire back through the bead and crimp, leaving a 3-in. (7.6cm) tail. Slide the bead and crimp close to the clasp, leaving a small space. Mash the crimp firmly in the hole closest to the handle, which looks like a half moon. Hold the wires apart so one piece is on each side of the deep dent.

Figure 8: Put the dented crimp in the front hole of the pliers on end, and press as hard as you can. This rolls the crimp into a cylinder.

figure 9

figure 10

square stitch

Figure 9: String the required number of beads for the first row. Then string the first bead of the second row and go through the last bead of the first row and the first bead of the second row in the same direction. The new bead sits on top of the old bead and the holes are horizontal.

Figure 10: String the second bead of row 2 and go through the next-to-last bead of row 1. Continue through the new bead of row 2. Repeat this step for the entire row.

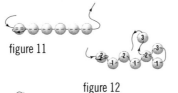

figure 11

figure 12

figure 13

even count flat peyote

Figure 11: String one bead and loop through it again in the same direction, leaving a 3-4-in. (8-10cm) tail. String beads to total an even number. These are the first two rows. (Remove the extra loop and weave the tail in later.)

Figure 12: Every other bead from **figure 11** drops down half a space to form row 1. To begin row 3 (count rows diagonally), pick up a bead and stitch through the second bead from the end. Pick up a bead and go through the fourth bead from the end. Continue in this manner. End by going through the first bead strung.

Figure 13: To start row 4 and all other rows, pick up a bead and go through the last bead added on the previous row.

Weave through the work in a zigzag path to end thread. Begin a thread the same way, exiting the last bead added in the same direction to resume.

right-angle weave

Figure 14: To start the first row, string 4 beads and tie into a snug circle. Pass the needle through the first 3 beads again.

Figure 15: Pick up 3 beads (#5, 6, and 7) and sew back through the last bead of the previous circle and #5 and 6.

Figure 16: Pick up 3 beads and sew back through #6 and the first 2 new beads. Continue adding 3 beads for each stitch until the first row is the desired length. You are sewing circles in a figure-8 and alternating direction with each stitch.

Figure 17: To begin row 2, sew through the last 3 beads of the last stitch on row 1, exiting the bead at the edge of one long side.

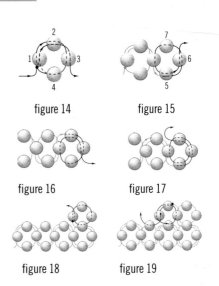

figure 14

figure 15

figure 16

figure 17

figure 18

figure 19

Figure 18: Pick up 3 beads and sew back through the bead you exited in **figure 17** (the first "top" bead of row 1) and the first new bead.

Figure 19: Pick up 2 beads and sew through the next top bead of the row below and the last bead of the previous stitch. Continue through the new beads and the next top bead on the row below.

Keep the thread moving in a figure-8. Pick up 2 beads for the remaining stitches on the row. Don't sew straight lines between stitches.

figure 20

figure 21

square knot

Figure 20: Bring the left-hand cord over the right-hand cord and around.

Figure 21: Cross right over left and go through the loop.

half-hitch knot

Figure 22: Come out a bead and form a loop perpendicular to the thread between beads. Bring the needle under the thread away from the loop. Then go back over the thread and through the loop. Pull gently so the knot doesn't tighten prematurely. ●

figure 22

Fab '50s

Inspired by a vintage 1950s bracelet, I used simple netting to create
an up-to-date bracelet. The technique used in this piece is easier
than it looks and goes very quickly once you get the pattern down.

❶ Thread a needle on 3 yd. (2.7m) of Fireline. String through 1 Japanese 10º triangle twice for a stopper bead and leave a 5-in. (12.7cm) tail. String *one 6mm round fire-polished bead (FP) and 3 triangles, repeating from * until you reach the desired length of your bracelet.

You've just created the center string of beads. The rest of the bracelet will be worked on either side of it.

❷ String half the toggle clasp and 3 triangles. Go back through last FP strung (**figure 1**).

❸ Going back toward the start, string 3 triangles between each FP bead for the length of the bracelet.

❹ String 3 triangles, the other half of the clasp, and 3 triangles. Go back through the first FP and the first two triangles from the next set of three (**figure 2, a-b**). Check the length and remove the stopper bead.

❺ String 7 triangles and go back through the second triangle from the next set of three (**b-c**). String 7 triangle beads between each second triangle for

the length of the bracelet.

❻ Go through the end 4 triangles that hold the clasp in place (**figure 3, a-b**), then string all the 7-triangle-bead loops on the other side of the bracelet (**b-c**).

❼ Go through the end 4 triangles holding the other half of the clasp in place, string the missing 7-triangle loop on the first side, and go through the first 4 beads in the next loop (**figure 4**).

❽ String 1 triangle bead, 1FP, and 1 triangle bead. Then go through the fourth triangle in the next 7-triangle loop (**figure 5**).

Continue adding 1 triangle bead, 1FP, and 1 triangle between each 7-triangle loop on the first side of the bracelet.

❾ After the last fourth triangle on the first side, go through 12 triangles to bring the thread around to the fourth triangle on the other side.

String 1 triangle, 1FP, and 1 triangle. Then go through the fourth triangle in the next 7-triangle loop.

Add 1 triangle, 1FP, and 1 triangle between each fourth triangle of the

7-triangle loops on the second side of the bracelet.

❿ Go through the 12 triangles on this end of the bracelet and string the final triangle bead, FP, and triangle bead set (**figure 6, a-b**).

⓫ Go through the next triangle bead, FP, and triangle bead set (**b-c**). String 3 triangles and go through the next triangle, FP, and triangle set (**c-d**). Continue this pattern around both sides of the bracelet.

⓬ Weave in the tails, tie several half-hitch knots between some of the beads in the bracelet (see "Basics," p. 2) and trim the tails. ⊙ – *Glenda Payseno*

---

materials – 8 in. (20cm) bracelet

- 6g Japanese size 10º triangles
- **37** 6mm Round fire-polished Czech glass beads
- Fireline, 6-lb.-test fishing line
- Toggle clasp
- Beading needles, #12

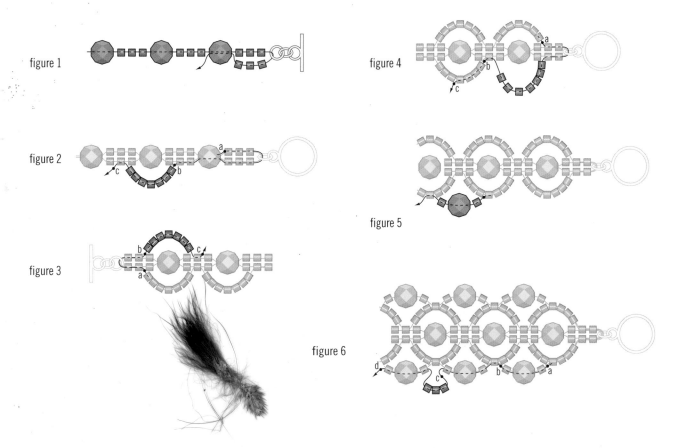

figure 1

figure 2

figure 3

figure 4

figure 5

figure 6

Flower and fringe ribbon

Contrast matte and shiny seed beads on a flat Ndebele
herringbone base. Then embellish the ends
with a flower clasp, crystals, and fringe.

begin the base

❶ Start with 3 yd. (2.7m) of thread. Use ladder stitch for the base (see "Basics," p. 2 and **figures 1-3**). String 2 size 8º seed beads. Leave a 10-in. (25cm) tail. Sew back up through the first bead from the tail end. Then go down the second bead (**figure 1**).

❷ Continue in ladder stitch for a total of four beads (**figures 2 and 3**).

❸ Zigzag back to the first bead, so the working thread and the tail exit opposite sides of it. The working thread exits the top of the bead and is on the left. You'll work left to right (or flip the work over and work right to left if you are left handed).

❹ Now switch to Ndebele stitch. String 2 size 8ºs. Go down the second bead and up the third bead in the previous row (**figure 4**).

❺ String 2 size 8ºs. Go down the fourth bead in the previous row (**figure 5**).

❻ String 1 triangle bead to turn the corner. Go up the last bead strung in the previous row (**figure 6**). Flip the work so the needle is on the left. Repeat from step 4 until the bracelet fits comfortably around your wrist. Leave the remaining thread to make a loop for the clasp.

create the clasp

❶ Weave the 10-in. starting tail up through 3 rows from the starting edge to exit a bead in one of the two middle columns so the flower or button will be flush with the first row (**figure 7, a-b**). String 1 size 11º seed bead, the flower, and an 11º. Go back through the flower and the first 11º. Sew back into the base on the other middle column (**b-c**). Repeat the thread path to reinforce the flower. Tie off the tail with half hitches (see "Basics") and trim.

❷ For the loop at the other end of the bracelet, bring the needle out the second bead in the last row (**figure 8, a-b**). Make a loop of 11ºs long enough to accommodate the flower clasp (mine is 24 beads long). Go down the third bead in the last row to complete the loop (**b-c**). Go back through the loop again to reinforce it.

❸ Bring the needle through the first 2 or 3 seed beads of the loop (**c-d**).

make the fringe

Alternate straight fringe with branched fringe every few seed beads on the loop.

❶ Straight fringe: Alternate 2 size 11ºs and a crystal 3 times. End with 3 size 11ºs. Skip the last 3 size 11ºs and go back through all the beads just added (**d-e**). Go through the next few seed beads in the loop.

❷ Branched fringe: String 3 size 11ºs, an 8º, 3 size 11ºs, a crystal, and 3 11ºs.

Skip the last 3 size 11ºs and go back through the crystal, and 3 11ºs (**e-f**).

Add 3 size 11ºs, a crystal, and 3 11ºs. Skip the last 3 11ºs and go back through the crystal, 3 11ºs, the 8º, and the first 3 11ºs (**f-g**). Go through the next few seed beads in the loop.

❸ Continue making fringe around the loop. Tie off the tail and trim. ●
– *Anna Nehs*

materials

- 10g Seed beads, size 8º, for bracelet and fringe
- 6g Triangle beads, size 10º, for bracelet
- 2g Seed beads, size 11º for fringe
- **40** (approx.) 4mm Austrian crystals or fire-polished, faceted beads
- Silamide or Fireline (6-lb.-test)
- Beading needles, #12
- Flat flower bead for clasp (from Eclectica, 262-641-0910) or use a 2-hole button

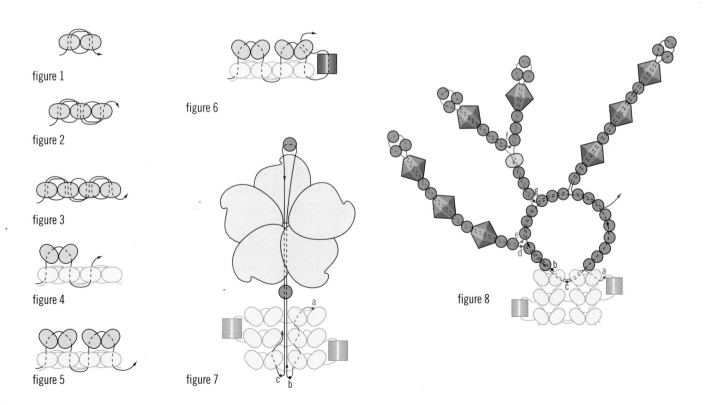

figure 1

figure 2

figure 3

figure 4

figure 5

figure 6

figure 7

figure 8

clasp

When the desired length is reached, sew half the clasp to that end. Weave kisses over the crystals and then sew the other half of the clasp to the other end of the bracelet.

To add the first clasp part, exit the last crystal, string 9AC cylinder beads and the clasp. Go through the opposite side of the last crystal (**photo d**). Reinforce by going through the added beads twice more. End exiting the last crystal.

kisses

❶ String 2MC cylinders, 1AC, and 2MC. Go through the crystal on the long side opposite where the thread exits, pointing the needle toward the clasp (**photo e**).
❷ String 2MC and go through the AC from step 1. String 2MC and go through the next vertical crystal (**photo f**).
❸ Repeat steps 1-2 to make kisses over the crystals until you reach the other end of the bracelet. Then add the other clasp part like the first.
❹ Weave in the tails, tie off with half-hitch knots (see "Basics"), and trim. ●
– Rachel Zash

materials

- **100** (approx.) 4mm Bicone Austrian crystals for an 8 in. (20cm) bracelet
- 3g Main color (MC) Japanese cylinder beads (Delicas)
- 1g Accent color (AC) Japanese cylinder beads
- 1 Lobster claw clasp with **2** split rings
- Fireline, 6-lb.-test or Silamide
- Beading needles, #12

Hugs & kisses bracelet

This bracelet begins with right-angle weave crystal circles, the hugs (see "Basics," p. 2 and **photos a-c**). Then you weave X's, kisses, of seed beads on top of the hugs.

When using any kind of thread with crystals, always pull it straight through the crystal, not against the edge, which is sometimes sharp.

hugs

❶ Thread the needle with 3 yd. (2.7m) of Fireline.
❷ String 4 crystals to the end of the thread, leaving a 10-in. (25cm) tail.
❸ Tie a square knot (see "Basics") so the crystals form a tight circle (**photo a**). Then go through the next 2 crystals again.

❹ String 3 crystals and go through the opposite side of the crystal that the thread exits (**photo b**).
❺ Go through 2 crystals so the thread comes out the side opposite the starting point (**photo c**). Keep the circles of crystals snug.
❻ Repeat steps 4 and 5 to the desired length.

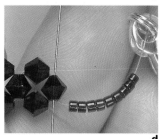

Stacked diamonds

Weave these earrings from the middle to the ends as you learn decreasing and increasing brick stitch (see "Basics," p. 2). Row and color layout are shown in the illustration on page 10.

materials
- **78** Main color (MC) Japanese seed beads, size 11º or Japanese cylinder beads (Delicas)
- **60** Accent color (AC) Japanese seed beads, size 11º or Japanese cylinder beads (Delicas)
- **4** 4mm Austrian crystals
- **2** 4mm Soldered jump rings
- **2** Ear wires
- Nymo D
- Beading needles, #12

decrease rows

❶ Thread a needle on 1 yd. (.9m) of Nymo D. Use ladder stitch (see "Basics," p. 2) to make the first 5-bead row, alternating 1AC and 1MC. Leave a 16-in. (41cm) tail.

❷ For row 2, string 1AC and 1MC and work as in "Basics," figure 4. String 1MC, go under the thread between the next two beads in row 1, and go up through the new MC ("Basics," figure 5). Repeat with 1AC.

❸ Work row 3 like row two, adding 3 beads and following the color pattern in the **figure** on p. 10.

❹ Work row 4 like the start of row 2 with 2MC beads.

increase rows

❶ For row 5, string 1MC and 1AC, go under the thread between the two beads in row 4, and go up the new AC. String 1MC, go under the same thread in row 4, and come back up the new MC.

❷ On row 6, string 1MC and 1AC, go under the thread between the first two beads in row 5, and go up through the new AC. String 1AC and work like figure 5 in "Basics." End the row with 1MC added to the same loop.

❸ Start row 7 like row 6, with 1MC and 1AC. String 1MC, go under the thread between the next two beads in row 6, and back up the new MC. String 1AC, go under the thread between the last two beads and back up the new AC. Finish the row with 1MC added to the same loop.

keep on stacking

❶ Continue by using the decrease directions for rows 8-10 and following the color pattern shown on p. 10. Exit the last MC bead added.

(continued next page)

2 String 1MC, a crystal, 1MC, and a jump ring. Go back down the MC, crystal, and MC (**figure, a-b**). Weave the thread into the diamond just completed. Tie off the thread with half-hitch knots (see "Basics") and trim the tails.

3 Flip the work over to repeat rows 2-10 on the other side of row 1, using the starting tail.

4 End with 1MC, a crystal, and 3MC. Go back through the crystal and the first MC (**figure, c-d**).

5 Finish this tail as in step 2. ●

– Anna Nehs

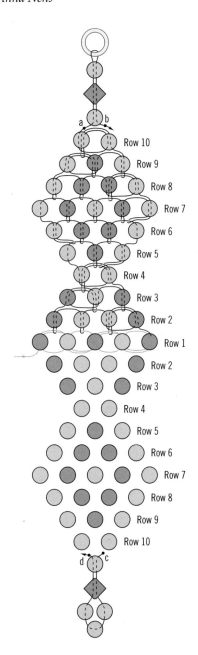

Endless Ndebele cuff

Using different shapes and finishes of beads creates a deceptively complicated look in this flat Ndebele herringbone cuff. But it's really easy to stitch and works up quickly.

making the base

1 Thread a needle with 3 yd. (2.7m) of Fireline. Make a ladder (see "Basics," p. 2 and **figures 1-3**), alternating a square and a triangle bead twice (4 beads). Leave a 6-in. (15cm) tail.

2 Flip the work so that the working thread comes out of the top of the last triangle on the left (lefties, work right to left).

3 String a square and a triangle. Take the needle down through the second bead and up through the third in the previous row (**figure 4**).

4 Add a square and a triangle. Take the needle down through the fourth bead (a square) in the previous row (**figure 5**).

5 String 2 size 11º seed beads to turn the corner and go up through the last triangle in the new row (**figure 6**).

6 Flip the work so that the triangle bead is on the left as the first bead in the new row. Repeat from step 3 until the bracelet fits around the widest part of your hand.

joining the ends

1 Connect the ends by weaving the tail from the end of the bracelet

figure 1

figure 2

figure 3

figure 4

figure 5

figure 6

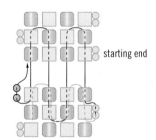

starting end

figure 7

into the first few rows of the beginning of the bracelet. Then weave the tail from the beginning into the last few rows of the end. Make sure the alternating triangle/square pattern matches up.

❷ The square at the edge of the last row will not have 2 size 11º seed beads next to it. Add these beads as you weave the ends together (**figure 7**). Weave in the tails and tie off, using half hitches (see "Basics"). Trim the tails.

filling in the gaps

❶ Thread a needle with 3 yd. of thread and come up through any edge square.

❷ Add 1 size 11º bead and go down through the next triangle in same row.

❸ Add 1 size 11º and go up through the next square in the same row.

❹ Add 1 size 11º bead and go down through the last triangle in the same row. Now pass the needle down the 2 size 11º beads on the edge and up through the square on the next row below (**figure 8, a-b**).

❺ Repeat from step 2 (**b-c**) until all of the spaces are filled. Weave the thread in and tie off as above. Then trim the tails. ❂ *– Anna Nehs*

materials

- 5-7g Japanese cube beads, 4mm
- 5-7g Japanese triangle beads, size 5º
- 5-7g Japanese seed beads, size 11º
- Fireline 6-lb.-test fishing line
- Beading needles, #10

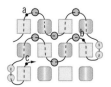

figure 8

Crisscross bracelet

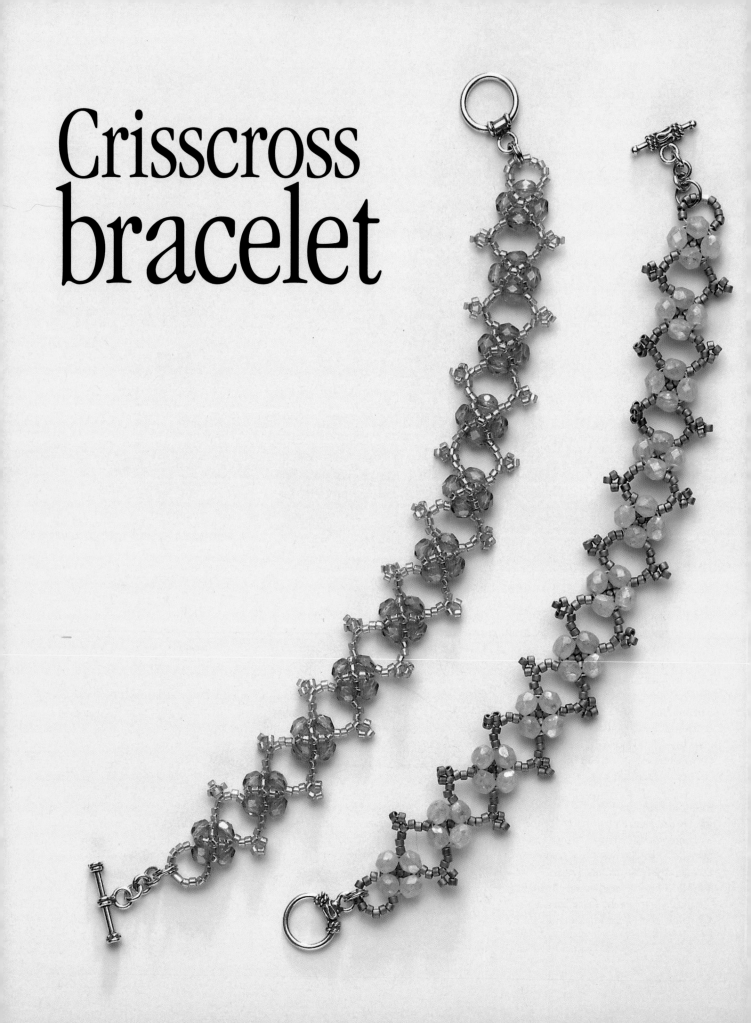

a

d

g

b

e

h

c

f

materials

- 2g Japanese cylinder beads (Delicas) or Japanese seed beads, size 11º
- Flexible beading wire (.012)
- 40-48 4mm Czech fire-polished, faceted beads
- 2 Split rings
- Toggle clasp
- 1 Crimp bead

Tools: diagonal wire cutter, crimping pliers or chainnose pliers; split ring pliers optional

I love the ease of making right-angle weave with the two-needle technique. The problem is that bead thread is not sturdy enough to support this design, so I substituted flexible beading wire for the thread. Now my beautiful bracelet is sturdy and easy to make without thread or needles.

crisscross cluster

❶ Prepare the clasp by attaching a split ring to each end.

❷ String 11 Japanese cylinder beads and one clasp part to the center of 2 yd. (1.8m) of flexible beading wire.

❸ Cross both strands through a 4mm fire-polished (FP) bead (**photo a**).

❹ String 1 FP on each strand and cross the wires through a fourth FP (**photo b**). Bring the strands back through the side FP beads. Then cross them through the first FP of the group again (**photo c**).

❺ On each strand, string 2 cylinder beads. Then cross them through another cylinder bead (**photo d**).

❻ On each strand, string 2 more cylinder beads and cross them through the fourth FP (**photo e**).

cluster connectors

❶ On each strand, string 7 cylinder beads. Skip the last 3 cylinders and take the wire back through the fourth cylinder from the end (**photo f**) to form a loop. Add 3 cylinders to each strand and cross the strands through 1 FP (**photo g**).

❷ Alternate crisscross clusters and connectors to the desired length. End with a crisscross cluster.

finishing touches

❶ String 5 cylinder beads on each strand. Add the other half of the clasp and cross the strands through a crimp bead (**photo h**).

❷ Bring one strand through the 5 cylinder beads, the end FP, the other 5 cylinders and the crimp to reinforce the loop. Take the other strand through 5 cylinders, if possible.

❸ Crimp the crimp bead (see "Basics," p. 2) and trim the tails. ❂ – *Anna Nehs*

Window bracelet

Square stitch looks just like loom weaving, but you do it without a loom. For this easy bracelet, you alternate sections of solid square stitch with four-row-high openings. Before resuming solid square stitch, you sew a 6mm bead into the center of the opening.

band

❶ Thread a beading needle with 2 yd. (1.8m) of waxed or conditioned thread. Pick up 1 cylinder bead and go through it again in the same direction for a stop bead. Leave a 12-in. (30cm) tail. String 10 main color (MC) cylinder beads.

❷ Pick up 2MC and go through the last 2 beads on the row below. Go back through the 2 new beads. Continue square stitching 2 beads at a time (**figure 1** and "Basics," p. 2). Work 4 MC rows.

❸ For row 5, square stitch 2MC, 6AC (accent color), and 2MC.

❹ Begin the first side of a window: Square stitch 2MC then 1AC. On the next row stitch 1AC and 1MC above the first two beads then 1MC. Repeat this pattern, adding two beads in the first stitch and one in the second for 4 rows (**figure 2, left side**).

❺ After adding the 3 beads on row 5, string 5AC and 2MC (**photo a**).

❻ Work four rows below the 3 edge beads (**photo b** and **figure 2, right side**).

❼ Square stitch the 3-bead side of the window to the three edge beads on the row below (**figure 3, a-b**).

❽ Zigzag through the first 2 rows on the right-hand side (**b-c**). String a 6mm bead and sew through the third row on the left-hand side (**c-d**). Sew through the second row, the 6mm bead, and the third row on the right (**d-e**). Repeat the thread path to reinforce the 6mm bead.

❾ Zigzag through the fourth row and the 3 edge beads on the top row (**e-f**). Repeat steps 2-9, ending with 4 MC

rows when the bracelet fits your wrist.

End short thread by zigzagging through a few beads on several rows. To add thread, retrace the last 3-5 stitches, exiting the last new bead.

finishing

❶ Taper the end as follows: Sew through the 2 end beads on the next-to-last row (**figure 4, a-b**), then go through 2 more beads on the last row (**b-c**). Square stitch 6 beads over the middle 6 of the last row (**c-d**).

❷ To add the button clasp, go through the last 3 beads (**d-e**). String 1 bead and go through the loop on the button and the added bead. Go through the fourth bead on the short row (**e-f**). Sew through the two beads below the middle two on the short row and the third bead on the short row (**f-g**). Repeat the thread path several times to reinforce the button.

❸ Remove the stop bead from the starting end of the bracelet and repeat step 1 to taper the end.

❹ Sew all the way through the short row (**figure 5, a-b**). String enough beads to make a loop that will fit snugly over the button (**b-c**). Go through the short row again. Repeat the thread path 3-4 times to reinforce the loop.

❺ For the edging, start a new thread or continue with the button thread. Come out the edge bead of the last full-width row. Pick up 3AC and sew down the second edge bead (**figure 6, a-b**). Sew out the next bead (**b-c**) and repeat. Edge both sides. ◓ – Alice Korach

materials

- 7.5g Japanese cylinder beads (Delicas), main color (MC)
- 3g Cylinder beads, accent color (AC)
- **8-12** 6mm Fire-polished, faceted beads or round Austrian crystals
- **1** Small shank button
- Beading needles, #10 or 12
- Nymo D beading thread
- Beeswax or Thread Heaven conditioner

a

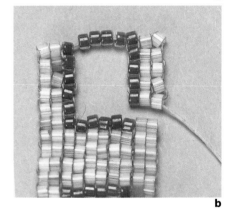

b

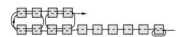

figure 1

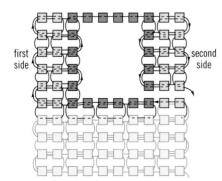

first side   second side

figure 2

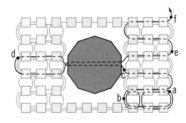

figure 3

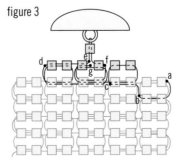

figure 4

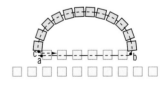

figure 5

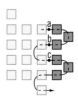

figure 6

Peyote bead bracelet

It's fun to use leftover seed beads to make even-count flat peyote beaded beads. They go fast and infinite variations are possible. You only need seven beaded beads and a few Austrian crystals for an 8½-in. (22cm) bracelet.

short beaded beads (make 4)

❶ Thread a needle with 24 in. (61cm) of bead thread. String a cylinder bead, an 11º seed bead, a 10º triangle, 2 size 8ºs, a 10º triangle, an 11º, and 2 cylinders. Leave an 8-in. (20cm) tail. These beads form the first two rows plus the first bead in the third row (see "Basics," p. 2).

② To begin row 3, skip the 2 cylinder beads and go through the 11º toward the tail (**figure 1**). Seat the cylinder beads next to each other.

③ Add a triangle, skip the triangle from step 1, and go through the first 8º.

④ Add an 8º, skip the second 8º, and go through the triangle. Add an 11º, skip the strung 11º, and go through the cylinder (**figure 2**).

⑤ Flip the work so you can keep sewing from bottom to top.

⑥ For row 4, add a cylinder and go through the new 11º. Add a triangle and go through the new 8º. Add an 8º and go through the new triangle. Add an 11º and go through the cylinder (**figure 3**).

⑦ Continue to flip work and add the matching bead in each space between the beads added on the previous row, until there are 5 cylinders along the top and the bottom (**figure 4**).

⑧ Roll the bead into a tube and sew the edges together, zigzagging back and forth between the high beads (**figure 5**).

⑨ When the tube is finished, weave the tails into it, tying several half-hitches (see "Basics") between beads. Trim the tails.

long beaded beads (make 3)

① Work the long bead like the short bead, but string 2 cylinders, 2 size 11ºs, 2 triangles, 2 size 8ºs, 2 triangles, 2 size 11ºs, and 3 cylinders for the first 2 rows (**figure 6**).

② Work the bead in peyote stitch, following **figures 7-9**.

③ When there are 5 beads along the top and bottom, roll the bead into a cylinder and zigzag the edges together (**figure 10**). End the tails as before.

assembly

① Crimp a toggle to one end of a 12-in. (30cm) length of flexible beading wire (see "Basics"). String a crystal, spacer, small peyote bead, spacer, crystal, spacer, long peyote bead, and a spacer (**photo**). Continue in this pattern to the desired length. ● – *Anna Nehs*

materials

About 100 of each style of seed bead:
- Japanese cylinder beads
- Size 11º seed beads
- Size 10º Japanese triangle beads
- Size 8º seed beads
- 14 4mm Silver spacers (2 per bead)
- 8 6mm Austrian crystals
- Toggle clasp
- 12 in. (30cm) Flexible beading wire, size .012-.015
- 2 Crimp beads
- Silamide beading thread or Fireline 6-lb.-test
- Beading needles, 10# or 12#

Tools: wire cutter, crimping pliers, scissors

figure 6

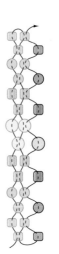

figure 7

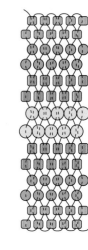

figure 8   figure 9

figure 1

figure 2

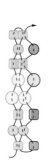

figure 3

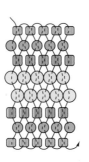

figure 4

last row

first row

figure 5

last row

figure 10

Crystal cuff

I originally tried using bead thread for this netted bracelet,
and planned to have a clasp. But every time I was about to finish,
the crystals cut the thread. So I decided to use flexible beading wire.
After weaving the band, I was thrilled to discover that the netting was
stretchy enough to fit over my hand in an endless design.